JENNIE BRUEN

CONVERSATIONAL FRENCH

French Phrase Book For Travelers

Contents

INTRODUCTION

Hello there! If you've got your sights set on visiting France or another French-speaking destination, you're in for an exciting adventure. France, with its captivating culture, rich history, and delectable cuisine, has a lot to offer.

Before you embark on your journey, here's a helpful tip: consider picking up some basic French. Even if it's just a handful of essential phrases, it can greatly enhance your travel experience.

This book is your gateway to acquiring conversational French that will serve you well in everyday scenarios. You'll discover how to greet people, introduce yourself, seek directions, order meals and beverages, and make purchases. Additionally, you'll gain insight into cultural nuances, such as tipping etiquette and restaurant dining customs.

Now, I understand what might be crossing your mind: "Learning a new language can be quite a challenge!" And you're absolutely right; it can be. But fear not, for I'm here to assist you. I've designed this book to be user-friendly, with clear and concise phrase explanations and plenty of examples to illustrate their usage.

So, what's stopping you? Dive into the world of conversational French today!

Here are a few handy tips to aid you on your language-learning journey:

1. Embrace your mistakes. Remember, everyone makes errors when learning a new language. The key is to keep practicing and learning from those slip-ups.
2. Immerse yourself in the language. Watch French movies and TV shows, listen to French music, and explore French literature. Seek opportunities to converse with native speakers.
3. Seek assistance when needed. If you find yourself struggling with a particular phrase or concept, don't hesitate to reach out to a friend, teacher, or tutor for guidance.

Learning a new language may pose its challenges, but the rewards are immense. Particularly when you can use your newfound language skills to explore a foreign country and fully embrace its culture.

So, bon courage! (Good luck!) Enjoy your journey into the world of French!

TIPS FOR LEARNING AND USING THIS BOOK

Learning a new language, especially one as beautiful and nuanced as French, can be a rewarding experience. To help you make the most of your journey into conversational French, we've compiled some practical tips:

1. **Consistency is Key**: Dedicate regular time to learning. Even a short daily practice can yield better results than sporadic, intensive study sessions.
2. **Immerse Yourself**: Surround yourself with the language as much as possible. Listen to French music, watch French films, and try to think in French whenever you can.
3. **Interactive Learning**: Engage in conversations with native speakers. Language exchange partners, language learning apps, and online communities can be excellent resources.
4. **Use Technology**: Leverage language learning apps and resources. They often provide interactive lessons, pronunciation guides, and quizzes to reinforce your skills.
5. **Set Realistic Goals**: Define achievable language goals for your trip. Whether it's mastering basic greetings or holding a conversation about your interests, having goals keeps you motivated.
6. **Practice Pronunciation**: Pay attention to pronunciation early on. Mimicking native speakers and using language learning apps with voice recognition can help refine your accent.
7. **Learn the Culture**: Understanding French culture, customs, and etiquette will make your interactions smoother and more enjoyable. It's more than just words; it's about connecting on a deeper level.
8. **Don't Fear Mistakes**: Mistakes are a natural part of language learning. Embrace them as opportunities to learn and improve. Native speakers appreciate your effort.
9. **Review and Repetition**: Regularly revisit what you've learned. Repetition helps solidify your memory and flu-

ency.

10. **Travel Prepared**: Before your trip, familiarize yourself with common travel phrases and specific vocabulary related to your itinerary.

11. **Use This Book Effectively**: This book provides structured lessons and essential phrases. Take advantage of the exercises and cultural insights within each chapter.

12. **Cultural Sensitivity**: Be respectful of cultural differences. Learn about local customs and gestures to avoid unintentional misunderstandings.

13. **Enjoy the Journey**: Learning a language is not just a means to an end; it's an enriching experience. Embrace the joy of communicating in French, even if it's just a few words.

Remember that learning a new language is a journey, and it's okay to progress at your own pace. By following these tips and staying committed to your learning goals, you'll be well-prepared to navigate and enjoy your travels in French-speaking regions. Bonne chance!

EFFECTIVE STRATEGIES FOR LANGUAGE ACQUISITION

Language acquisition is an exciting journey, and mastering conversational French for your travels requires effective strategies. Here are some proven methods to accelerate your learning process:

1. **Immerse Yourself**: Surround yourself with the French language as much as possible. Change your phone and social media settings to French, watch French TV shows

and movies, and read books or articles in French. The more exposure you have, the quicker you'll pick up the language.

2. **Start with the Basics**: Begin with essential phrases, greetings, and common expressions. These provide a strong foundation for effective communication and build your confidence.

3. **Use Language Learning Apps**: There are numerous language learning apps available, such as Duolingo, Rosetta Stone, and Babbel. These apps offer structured lessons, interactive exercises, and pronunciation practice.

4. **Practice Speaking**: Conversational practice is crucial. Engage in conversations with native speakers whenever possible. Language exchange partners, language learning communities, and online language tutors can provide valuable speaking opportunities.

5. **Set Specific Goals**: Define clear language goals for your travels. For example, aim to order a meal in French, ask for directions, or engage in a short conversation. Setting achievable goals keeps you motivated.

6. **Listen Actively**: Pay attention to how native speakers pronounce words and phrases. Mimicking their intonation and rhythm can help improve your pronunciation.

7. **Read Aloud**: Reading French texts aloud helps reinforce your pronunciation and fluency. Start with simple texts and gradually work your way up to more complex material.

8. **Keep a Language Journal**: Maintain a journal where you jot down new words, phrases, and cultural insights you encounter. Reviewing this journal regularly reinforces your learning.

9. **Join Language Classes**: Enrolling in formal language classes or workshops can provide structured learning and

the guidance of an experienced instructor.

10. **Watch French Films and TV**: Watching French-language content with subtitles can improve your listening skills and expose you to colloquial language.

11. **Use Flashcards**: Create flashcards with French words or phrases on one side and their English equivalents on the other. Review them regularly to expand your vocabulary.

12. **Practice with Native Speakers**: Conversing with native speakers not only enhances your language skills but also offers cultural insights. Look for language exchange partners or language meetup groups in your area or online.

13. **Stay Consistent**: Consistency is key to language acquisition. Dedicate a set amount of time each day to practice and stick to your schedule.

14. **Reward Yourself**: Celebrate your language milestones, whether it's completing a chapter in this book or successfully holding a conversation with a native speaker. Rewards can motivate you to continue learning.

15. **Embrace Mistakes**: Don't fear making mistakes. Learning from errors is an integral part of the language acquisition process.

FACTS YOU NEED TO KNOW ABOUT FRENCH

Let's dive into some intriguing facts about the French language:

1. French, a Romance language, traces its roots back to Latin. It boasts a vast community of speakers, with over 274 million people worldwide, ranking it as the sixth most

spoken language globally.

2. French holds the official language status in 29 countries, including France, Canada, Belgium, Switzerland, and several African nations. Additionally, it serves as one of the official languages for significant international bodies like the United Nations, the European Union, and the African Union.

3. French is a favored choice for second language acquisition. It's considered relatively accessible for English speakers, making it an attractive option for language learners.

4. French is renowned for its beauty and expressiveness. Its extensive vocabulary and intricate grammar rules contribute to its allure.

5. The language boasts a rich diversity. Various French dialects are spoken worldwide, each carrying its distinctive features.

Now, let us go deeper into the world of French with some additional insights:

1. French holds the title of the "language of love and romance." It is closely associated with the romantic ambiance of Paris, along with its delectable cuisine.

2. The language plays a pivotal role in the realms of fashion and art. Paris stands as a global hub for renowned fashion houses and art museums.

3. French is deeply entrenched in the domains of science and technology. France boasts a legacy of scientific innovation, with many French scientists and engineers leaving indelible marks on the world.

4. The language of diplomacy and international relations,

French enjoys prominence as one of the official languages of the United Nations. It's commonly employed in various international negotiations and agreements.

Embarking on the journey of learning French can unlock a multitude of opportunities. It facilitates easier travel, enhances job prospects, and enables connections with individuals from diverse corners of the globe.

So, why not embark on your French learning adventure today?

CHAPTER 1

GREETINGS AND INTRODUCTIONS

BASIC GREETINGS

At the core of any successful interaction in French-speaking regions are the basic greetings. These words and phrases set the tone for your conversation and convey your respect and friendliness. Here's an in-depth look at some common French greetings:

1. **Bonjour** - This versatile greeting means "Good morning" or simply "Hello." It's used from the early morning hours until around noon. When you say "Bonjour," you're not just acknowledging the time of day; you're extending goodwill and politeness.

2. **Bonsoir** - As the day turns into evening, the appropriate greeting shifts to "Bonsoir," which means "Good evening." You can use it when you arrive at a social event, enter a restaurant for dinner, or simply meet someone in the evening hours. Like "Bonjour," it carries an air of politeness and courtesy.

3. **Salut** - When you're among friends, peers, or acquaintances in an informal setting, "Salut" is a casual and friendly way to say "Hi" or "Hello." It's akin to a warm wave or nod of recognition. While it fosters familiarity, it's best avoided in more formal or business contexts.

4. **Coucou** - For an even more relaxed and informal greeting, you can use "Coucou." Think of it as the French equivalent of saying "Hey" in English. This expression is typically reserved for close friends and family members and conveys a sense of intimacy and affection.

5. **Bienvenue** - When you want to extend a warm welcome to someone, "Bienvenue" is the word to use. It means "Welcome" and is often employed when inviting someone into your home or expressing hospitality.

6. **Salutations** - If you're writing a formal letter or email, "Salutations" can be used as a polite way to begin your message. It's akin to saying "Greetings" or "Hello."

Remember that the choice of greeting in French is influenced by both the time of day and the level of formality in the situation. While "Bonjour" and "Bonsoir" are suitable for most scenarios, "Salut" and "Coucou" are reserved for informal or friendly encounters.

MASTERING THE ART OF SAYING HELLO

Saying "Hello" in any language is not just a linguistic act; it's a cultural exchange and a gesture of goodwill. To master the art of saying hello in French, consider these additional aspects:

1. **Smile**: A genuine smile transcends language barriers. It instantly communicates warmth and friendliness, making your greeting more effective.

2. **Eye Contact**: Maintaining eye contact when you greet someone is a sign of respect and attentiveness. It shows that you are engaged in the interaction.

3. **Using the Right Greeting**: Choosing the appropriate greeting is essential. "Bonjour" and "Bonsoir" are generally safe choices, but remember that using titles and last names (e.g., Monsieur, Madame) adds a layer of politeness and formality when necessary.

4. **Politeness Prevails**: When in doubt, opt for politeness, especially when meeting someone for the first time. Adding titles and last names, such as "Monsieur Dupont," is a courteous gesture that demonstrates respect.

5. **Pronunciation Matters**: Pay attention to the pronunciation of greetings. Accurate pronunciation not only boosts your confidence but also ensures that your greetings are clear and easily understood by native speakers.

INTRODUCING YOURSELF AND OTHERS

Introducing yourself and others is a fundamental part of any interaction. It's a gesture of politeness and creates a sense of inclusion. Let's delve into how you can effectively introduce yourself and others in French:

Introducing Yourself:

1. **Je m'appelle [Your Name]** - The most basic way to in-

troduce yourself is to say, "Je m'appelle [Your Name]," which means "My name is [Your Name]." For example, "Je m'appelle Marie" (My name is Marie).

2. **Je suis [Your Name]** - Another way to introduce yourself is to say, "Je suis [Your Name]," meaning "I am [Your Name]." For example, "Je suis Pierre" (I am Pierre).

3. **Enchanté(e)** - After introducing yourself, it's common to express your pleasure in meeting someone by saying "Enchanté" if you're male or "Enchantée" if you're female. This translates to "Nice to meet you" or "Delighted."

Introducing Others:

1. **Voici [Name]** - To introduce someone else, you can say "Voici [Name]," which means "This is [Name]." For instance, "Voici Anne" (This is Anne).

2. **Permettez-moi de vous présenter [Name]** - For a more formal introduction, you can say, "Permettez-moi de vous présenter [Name]," which means "Allow me to introduce [Name]." For example, "Permettez-moi de vous présenter Jean" (Allow me to introduce Jean).

BREAKING THE ICE IN FRENCH

Breaking the ice, especially in a foreign language, can be a bit daunting, but it's an essential skill for making connections and starting conversations.

1. **Begin with Greetings**: Start with a friendly "Bonjour" or "Bonsoir" based on the time of day. This sets a polite and

welcoming tone for your interaction.

2. **Use Compliments**: Compliments are a fantastic icebreaker. You can say something positive about the person's appearance or the environment. For example, "Votre robe est très élégante" (Your dress is very elegant) or "Cet endroit est magnifique" (This place is beautiful).

3. **Ask Open-Ended Questions**: Engage the other person by asking open-ended questions that invite conversation. For instance, "Qu'est-ce qui vous amène ici?" (What brings you here?) or "Qu'aimez-vous faire pendant votre temps libre?" (What do you like to do in your free time?).

4. **Share a Little About Yourself**: After introducing yourself, offer a bit of information about your interests or the reason for your presence. This encourages the other person to do the same.

5. **Practice Active Listening**: Pay close attention to the other person's responses. Active listening shows that you're genuinely interested in the conversation.

6. **Show Empathy**: Empathize with the other person's experiences or opinions. This fosters a sense of connection.

7. **Use Humor Wisely**: Humor can be a great icebreaker, but it's important to be culturally sensitive and avoid humor that may be misinterpreted.

Remember, breaking the ice is about creating a comfortable and friendly atmosphere. In French culture, politeness and respect go a long way, so embrace these qualities in your interactions.

With the skills to introduce yourself and others and the art of breaking the ice in French, you're well on your way to confident and engaging interactions in French-speaking regions.

ASKING QUESTIONS ABOUT SOMEONE

When you meet someone new or reconnect with acquaintances, asking questions about them is a great way to show interest and build rapport. Let us explore some common questions you can use to inquire about someone in French:

1. **Comment ça va ?** - A universal way to start a conversation is by asking, "Comment ça va ?" which means "How are you?" It's a friendly and polite inquiry into the other person's well-being.

2. **Comment vous appelez-vous ?** - If you want to know the person's name, you can ask, "Comment vous appelez-vous ?" This translates to "What is your name?" It's a formal way to inquire about someone's identity.

3. **Tu t'appelles comment ?** - For a more casual setting, you can ask, "Tu t'appelles comment ?" which means "What's your name?" This is a common way to ask someone's name among friends or peers.

4. **D'où venez-vous ?** - To learn more about their background, you can ask, "D'où venez-vous ?" meaning "Where are you from?" This question invites them to share their place of origin.

5. **Qu'est-ce que vous faites dans la vie ?** - If you're interested in their occupation, you can ask, "Qu'est-ce que vous faites dans la vie ?" This translates to "What do you do in life?" It's a polite way to inquire about their profession.

6. **Tu fais quoi dans la vie ?** - In a more casual context, you can ask, "Tu fais quoi dans la vie ?" which means "What do you do in life?" This is a common way to ask about someone's job or activities among friends.

7. **Quel est votre passe-temps préféré ?** - To delve into their hobbies and interests, you can ask, "Quel est votre passe-temps préféré ?" which means "What is your favorite pastime?" This question can lead to engaging conversations about shared interests.

8. **Tu aimes quoi comme passe-temps ?** - In informal settings, you can ask, "Tu aimes quoi comme passe-temps ?" which translates to "What hobbies do you like?" This question encourages a friendly discussion about leisure activities.

ENGAGING IN CONVERSATIONS

Engaging in conversations is about active participation and genuine interest in what the other person has to say. Here are some tips to enhance your conversational skills in French:

1. **Listen Actively**: Give the speaker your full attention. Show that you're actively listening by nodding and making appropriate verbal responses like "Je comprends" (I understand) or "C'est intéressant" (That's interesting).

2. **Ask Follow-Up Questions**: When someone shares something, ask follow-up questions to delve deeper into the topic. For example, if they mention a hobby, you can ask about their favorite aspects or experiences related to it.

3. **Share Your Thoughts**: Don't hesitate to share your opinions and experiences. It's a two-way conversation, and your perspective adds depth to the interaction.

4. **Use Transition Phrases**: Transition phrases like "D'ailleurs"

(By the way), "À propos" (Speaking of), and "En ce qui concerne" (Regarding) help smoothly move from one topic to another.

5. **Be Polite and Respectful**: Politeness is highly regarded in French culture. Use expressions like "S'il vous plaît" (Please) and "Merci" (Thank you) generously.

6. **Body Language**: Pay attention to your body language. Maintain eye contact, use open and inviting gestures, and avoid crossing your arms, which can appear defensive.

7. **Avoid Interrupting**: Let the speaker finish their thoughts before responding. Interrupting can be seen as impolite.

8. **Use Filler Words Sparingly**: While filler words like "euh" (um) exist in all languages, use them sparingly. Overusing filler words can make you appear less confident.

TAKING LEAVE

Knowing how to take leave gracefully is as crucial as starting a conversation. Whether you've had a brief encounter or a lengthy discussion.

some ways to say goodbye in French:

1. **Au revoir** – The most common way to bid farewell is by saying "Au revoir," which means "Goodbye." It's a polite and versatile phrase suitable for most situations.

2. **Salut** – If you're in an informal setting among friends or acquaintances, you can simply say "Salut" to say goodbye. It's a friendly and casual way to take your leave.

3. **À bientôt** – To express the hope of seeing someone again

soon, you can say "À bientôt," which means "See you soon." It conveys a sense of anticipation for the next meeting.

4. **À tout à l'heure** - If you're parting ways with the expectation of meeting again later the same day, you can say "À tout à l'heure," which means "See you later."

5. **À demain** - When parting in the evening with the expectation of meeting again the next day, you can say "À demain," which means "See you tomorrow."

6. **Bonne journée** - To wish someone a good day as you say goodbye, you can say "Bonne journée," which means "Have a good day."

7. **Bonne soirée** - In the evening, you can wish someone a good evening with "Bonne soirée," which means "Have a good evening."

Saying Goodbye Gracefully

Saying goodbye gracefully is not just about the words; it's also about the tone and body language.

some tips to say goodbye in a graceful and polite manner:

1. **Express Appreciation**: Show appreciation for the time spent together. You can say "Merci pour la conversation" (Thank you for the conversation) or "C'était un plaisir de vous rencontrer" (It was a pleasure to meet you).

2. **Use Appropriate Phrases**: Choose the goodbye phrase that suits the context and the level of familiarity with the person. "Au revoir" is a safe and polite choice for most situations.

3. **Maintain Eye Contact**: Maintain eye contact when saying goodbye. It conveys sincerity and respect.

4. **Offer a Handshake or Kiss on the Cheek**: In formal settings

or when parting with acquaintances, a firm handshake is appropriate. In more familiar settings, a kiss on each cheek is a common French custom for greetings and farewells.

5. **Smile**: A warm smile as you say goodbye leaves a positive impression and conveys friendliness.

6. **Avoid Rushing**: Take your time to say goodbye. Rushing can make it seem like you're eager to leave, which may come across as impolite.

7. **Use the Appropriate Level of Formality**: Adjust your tone and choice of words based on the level of formality in the situation. "Au revoir" is suitable for most situations, while "Salut" is more casual.

By using appropriate phrases and gestures and expressing appreciation, you can say goodbye gracefully in French, leaving a positive impression on the people you meet.

CHAPTER 2

GETTING AROUND

ASKING FOR DIRECTIONS

Navigating unfamiliar places can be an adventure, but it's essential to know how to ask for directions when you need guidance.

1. **Excusez-moi, pouvez-vous m'indiquer le chemin vers [Place/Location]?** - This polite phrase means "Excuse me, can you show me the way to [Place/Location]?" Use it when seeking specific directions.

2. **Où est [Place/Location]?** - For a more straightforward inquiry, you can simply ask, "Où est [Place/Location]?" which means "Where is [Place/Location]?"

3. **Je suis perdu(e)** - If you're lost and need assistance, you can say, "Je suis perdu" if you're male or "Je suis perdue" if you're female, which means "I am lost." This can prompt locals to offer help.

4. **Comment puis-je aller à [Place/Location]?** - To ask how to get to a specific place, you can say, "Comment puis-je

aller à [Place/Location]?" which means "How can I go to [Place/Location]?"

5. **Est-ce que vous pourriez m'indiquer le chemin vers [Place/Location]?** - This is a more formal way to ask for directions. It means "Could you please show me the way to [Place/Location]?"

6. **Pouvez-vous me montrer sur la carte?** - If you have a map and want someone to point out the location, you can ask, "Pouvez-vous me montrer sur la carte?" which means "Can you show me on the map?"

7. **Est-ce loin d'ici?** - To inquire about the distance to a place, you can ask, "Est-ce loin d'ici?" which means "Is it far from here?"

8. **Je cherche [Place/Location]** - If you're actively searching for a place, you can say, "Je cherche [Place/Location]," which means "I'm looking for [Place/Location]."

Finding Your Way with Confidence

Navigating a new city or area can be an empowering experience.

1. **Carry a Map or Use GPS**: A map or GPS app on your phone can be invaluable. It allows you to visualize your route and landmarks.

2. **Learn Basic Directions**: Familiarize yourself with basic directional terms like "droite" (right), "gauche" (left), "tout droit" (straight ahead), and "derrière" (behind).

3. **Use Landmarks**: Look for prominent landmarks like monuments, churches, or major buildings. These can serve as reference points when asking for directions.

4. **Ask Locals**: Don't hesitate to ask locals for help. Most

people are willing to assist travelers, and it can lead to meaningful interactions.

5. **Learn Numbers and Street Names**: Knowing numbers and street names in French can help you understand directions better.

6. **Plan Ahead**: Before venturing out, plan your route and have a general sense of the landmarks and streets you'll encounter.

7. **Be Courteous**: When asking for directions, begin with a polite greeting like "Bonjour" or "Excusez-moi" and express gratitude with "Merci" (Thank you).

8. **Stay Calm**: If you get lost, stay calm. It's all part of the adventure, and you'll likely discover new places along the way.

TAKING PUBLIC TRANSPORTATION

Public transportation is often a convenient and eco-friendly way to get around in cities and regions. Here's what you need to know about taking public transportation in French-speaking areas:

Riding Buses, Trains, and Trams

1. **Bus (Autobus)**:

- **Bus Stop (Arrêt de bus)**: Look for signs indicating bus stops. You can ask someone, "Où est l'arrêt de bus?" (Where is the bus stop?).

- **Bus Ticket (Billet de bus)**: Tickets can be purchased at kiosks, machines, or directly from the bus driver. You can say, "Un billet, s'il vous plaît" (A ticket, please).
- **Bus Schedule (Horaires de bus)**: Check the bus schedule (horaires de bus) to know when the next bus arrives. You might ask, "Quand arrive le prochain bus?" (When does the next bus arrive?).
- **Bus Routes (Lignes de bus)**: Familiarize yourself with bus routes (lignes de bus) to ensure you're on the right bus. You can ask, "Est-ce que ce bus va à [Destination]?" (Does this bus go to [Destination]?).

1. **Train (Train)**:

- **Train Station (Gare)**: Locate train stations (gares) in the city. You can inquire, "Où est la gare?" (Where is the train station?).
- **Train Ticket (Billet de train)**: Purchase train tickets (billets de train) from ticket counters or automated machines. You can request, "Un billet, s'il vous plaît" (A ticket, please).
- **Train Schedule (Horaires de train)**: Check the train schedule (horaires de train) to find departure times. You might ask, "À quelle heure part le prochain train pour [Destination]?" (What time does the next train to [Destination] leave?).
- **Train Platform (Quai de train)**: Look for signs indicating the train platform (quai de train) for your departure. You can ask, "Où est le quai pour le train [Destination]?" (Where is the platform for the [Destination] train?).

1. **Tram (Tramway)**:

- **Tram Stop (Arrêt de tramway)**: Find tram stops (arrêts de tramway) along the tram route. You can inquire, "Où est l'arrêt de tramway le plus proche?" (Where is the nearest tram stop?).
- **Tram Ticket (Billet de tramway)**: Purchase tram tickets (billets de tramway) from machines or at designated kiosks. You can say, "Un billet, s'il vous plaît" (A ticket, please).
- **Tram Schedule (Horaires de tramway)**: Check the tram schedule (horaires de tramway) to plan your journey. You might ask, "À quelle heure passe le prochain tram pour [Destination]?" (What time does the next tram to [Destination] pass?).
- **Tram Route (Ligne de tramway)**: Be aware of tram routes (lignes de tramway) and ensure you're on the correct tram. You can inquire, "Ce tramway va-t-il à [Destination]?" (Does this tram go to [Destination]?).

Additional Tips for Public Transportation:

- **Validate Tickets**: Some transportation systems require you to validate your ticket before boarding. Look for validation machines.
- **Keep Your Ticket**: Always keep your ticket until the end of your journey, as ticket inspections may occur.
- **Ask for Help**: Don't hesitate to ask transportation staff or fellow passengers if you need assistance. You can say, "Pouvez-vous m'aider, s'il vous plaît?" (Can you help me, please?).

BUYING TICKETS

When using public transportation in French-speaking areas, it's important to know how to purchase tickets for buses, trains, trams, and other modes of transit.

1. Ticket Counters (Guichets):

- **Locating the Counter**: Ticket counters (guichets) are typically found at train stations, bus terminals, and major transit hubs. Look for signs that say "Guichets" or "Billetterie."
- **Queue Up**: Join the queue (la file d'attente) if there are others waiting. You might hear people saying "La queue, s'il vous plaît" (The line, please) to maintain order.
- **Select Your Service**: Once at the counter, the agent may ask, "Comment puis-je vous aider?" (How can I help you?). Specify your destination and any preferences, such as one-way or round-trip tickets.
- **Payment**: Pay for your ticket using cash, credit card, or other accepted methods. Be sure to have the necessary currency or payment card ready.
- **Ask for Information**: Don't hesitate to ask for additional information about schedules, seat reservations, or any discounts that may apply to your journey.
- **Receive Your Ticket**: Once the payment is processed, the agent will provide you with your ticket. Verify that the details, such as the departure time and destination, are correct.

2. Automated Ticket Machines (Automates de billetterie):

- **Locating Machines**: Automated ticket machines (auto-mates de billetterie) are often found at transportation hubs, including train stations and tram stops. Look for the machine labeled "Billetterie" or "Tickets."
- **Select Language**: Many machines offer language options. Choose the language you're most comfortable with.
- **Choose Your Ticket Type**: The machine will typically present options for different ticket types, such as one-way, round-trip, or daily passes. Select the one that suits your needs.
- **Specify Destination**: Enter your destination. Some machines have touchscreens, while others use buttons to input information.
- **Payment**: Follow the prompts to make your payment. Most machines accept cash, coins, and credit cards. Ensure you have the correct amount or payment card.
- **Check for Discounts**: Some machines offer discounts for children, seniors, or students. If applicable, select the appropriate discount category.
- **Collect Your Ticket**: After payment, the machine will dispense your ticket. Verify that the information, including the date and destination, is accurate.

3. Validating Your Ticket (Validation):

- **Before Boarding**: Some public transportation systems require you to validate your ticket before boarding. Validation machines are often located near the platforms or inside vehicles.
- **Insert and Stamp**: Insert your ticket into the validation machine, and it will stamp the date and time. This ensures

your ticket is valid for the journey.

- **Keep Your Ticket**: Hold onto your ticket throughout your trip, as ticket inspections may occur, and you may need it to exit some stations.

RENTING A CAR

Renting a car provides you with the flexibility to explore regions at your own pace, especially when public transportation may not be readily available.

1. Choosing a Rental Company (Choisir une Agence de Location):

- **Research**: Begin by researching rental car companies in the area you plan to visit. Look for reputable companies with good reviews and competitive rates.
- **Book in Advance**: It's often advisable to book your rental car in advance, especially during peak travel seasons. Online reservations are convenient and allow you to compare prices.
- **Consider Pickup Location**: Choose a pickup location that is convenient for your travel plans, such as an airport, train station, or city center office.

2. Required Documents (Documents Requis):

- **Driver's License (Permis de Conduire)**: Ensure that you have a valid driver's license. In most cases, an international driver's license is not necessary, but check the requirements of the rental company and the local regulations.

· **Identification (Pièce d'Identité)**: Carry a valid identification document, such as a passport or national ID card, as rental companies may require it.

· **Credit Card (Carte de Crédit)**: Have a credit card in your name for payment and deposit purposes. Some rental companies may also accept debit cards.

3. Booking and Reservation (Réservation):

· **Online Booking**: Use the rental company's website or a trusted online booking platform to reserve your car. Provide all necessary information, including pickup and drop-off times and locations.

· **Vehicle Selection**: Choose the type of car that suits your needs, whether it's a compact, sedan, SUV, or other options. Consider factors like the number of passengers and luggage.

· **Optional Extras**: Rental companies often offer additional services like GPS, child seats, and insurance packages. Decide if you need any of these extras and include them in your reservation.

4. Pickup and Inspection (Prise en Charge et Inspection):

· **Arrival**: On the designated day, arrive at the rental car pickup location at the specified time. Have your reservation confirmation, driver's license, identification, and credit card ready.

· **Vehicle Inspection**: Before accepting the car, inspect it thoroughly for any existing damage, such as dents or scratches.

Note any issues on the rental agreement or take photos as evidence.

- **Documentation**: Review the rental agreement carefully. Ensure that you understand the terms, including fuel policy, mileage limits, and any potential fees.

5. Driving and Navigation (Conduite et Navigation):

- **Local Driving Rules**: Familiarize yourself with the local driving rules, including speed limits, road signs, and parking regulations. In France, for example, you drive on the right side of the road.
- **GPS or Navigation**: Consider using a GPS device or a navigation app on your phone to help you navigate the roads. Ensure that the device is set to your preferred language.
- **Fuel**: Gasoline (essence) and diesel (gazole) are commonly available in French-speaking regions. Pay attention to fuel types and choose the one compatible with your rental car.

6. Returning the Car (Rendre la Voiture):

- **Return Time**: Return the car at the agreed-upon time and location. Late returns may result in additional charges.
- **Fuel Level**: Fill up the gas tank to the level specified in the rental agreement. If you return the car with less fuel, you may incur refueling charges.
- **Inspection**: Allow the rental company's staff to inspect the vehicle. Ensure that there are no new damages beyond what was noted during pickup.
- **Return Documents**: Return the keys, rental agreement, and any rental car accessories or equipment provided.

GETTING A TAXI

Taxis are a convenient mode of transportation in many French-speaking regions, especially for short trips or when public transportation may not be readily available.

1. Identifying Taxis (Identifier les Taxis):

- **Taxi Signs**: Look for vehicles with official taxi signs on top. In France, for example, taxis typically have a taxi sign that's illuminated when they're available for hire.
- **Taxi Ranks (Station de Taxis)**: Taxi ranks are designated areas where taxis queue up for passengers. You can often find them at transportation hubs, hotels, and popular tourist areas.

2. Hailing a Taxi (Héler un Taxi):

- **Raising Your Hand**: To signal a taxi, stand at the curb and raise your arm. It's a universal gesture for hailing a cab.
- **Look for an Available Taxi**: Ensure that the taxi's illuminated sign on top is lit, indicating that it's available for hire.
- **Queue at Taxi Ranks**: If you're at a taxi rank, simply wait in line for the next available taxi.

3. Communicating with the Driver (Communiquer avec le Chauffeur):

- **Address**: Provide the driver with the address of your destination. You can say, "À [Destination], s'il vous plaît" (To [Destination], please).

- **Language**: It's helpful to know some basic French phrases for communication, but many taxi drivers in tourist areas speak English or other languages.
- **Ask for Receipt**: If you need a receipt (reçu), you can say, "Un reçu, s'il vous plaît" (A receipt, please).

4. Payment (Paiement):

- **Metered Fare**: Taxis in French-speaking regions typically have meters. The fare is calculated based on distance traveled and waiting time.
- **Payment Methods**: Taxis usually accept cash and credit cards. Confirm with the driver before starting the trip, especially if you plan to pay with a card.
- **Tipping**: Tipping is customary but not obligatory. You can round up the fare or add a small tip as a gesture of appreciation. For example, if the fare is €9.50, you can give €10.

5. Taxi Apps (Applications de Taxi):

- **Ride-Hailing Apps**: In some French-speaking regions, ride-hailing apps like Uber operate. You can use these apps to book and pay for taxi rides.

6. Safety (Sécurité):

- **Official Taxis**: Use official and licensed taxis to ensure safety and reliability.
- **License and Identification**: Taxis should display a license and the driver's identification inside the vehicle.

- **Check Fare**: Confirm with the driver that the meter is running before the trip begins to avoid disputes over the fare.

7. Taxi Services (Services de Taxi):

- **Airport Taxis**: Many airports have dedicated taxi services with fixed rates to various destinations. Inquire at the airport information desk.
- **Hotels and Restaurants**: Hotels and restaurants can often help you arrange for a taxi. They can also provide you with information on typical fares to specific destinations.

By following these steps and guidelines, you can easily get a taxi and hail a cab in French-speaking regions, ensuring a convenient and safe way to travel within the area

CHAPTER 3

ACCOMMODATION

CHECKING IN AND OUT OF A HOTEL

Checking In at a Hotel:

1. **Arrival**: When you arrive at the hotel, it's essential to be courteous. Approach the front desk with a warm greeting. Depending on the time of day, you can say, "Bonjour" (Good morning) or "Bonsoir" (Good evening). This polite gesture sets a friendly tone for your interaction.

2. **Reservation**: If you've made a reservation in advance, inform the hotel staff by saying, "J'ai une réservation au nom de [Your Name]" (I have a reservation under the name of [Your Name]). This allows the staff to locate your booking quickly. It's helpful to have your reservation confirmation or a printout ready, as well as your ID.

3. **Identification**: To check you in, the hotel staff will need to verify your identity. They might request your passport or ID, as well as a credit card for

any potential incidental charges during your stay. Hand over these documents as requested, ensuring they match the reservation details.

4. **Room Assignment**: After confirming your reservation and identification, the hotel staff will assign you a room. They may say, "Voici votre clé de chambre" (Here is your room key). They'll provide you with a physical key card or a key, depending on the hotel's setup. Make sure to ask about the location of your room and any relevant information about it.

5. **Payment**: If you haven't prepaid for your stay, you'll need to settle the payment at this point. Politely ask, "Combien ça coûte pour la nuit?" (How much does it cost per night?). The staff will provide you with the total amount. You can pay in cash or use your credit card. Ensure you receive a receipt for your records.

6. **Additional Information**: It's a good idea to inquire about the hotel's amenities and services. For example, you can ask, "Est-ce que le petit-déjeuner est inclus?" (Is breakfast included?). This way, you can plan your morning accordingly. You can also ask about Wi-Fi access, parking facilities, or any special services the hotel offers.

Checking Out of a Hotel:

1. **Departure**: When it's time to check out, visit the front desk and let them know you'd like to settle your bill. You can say, "Je souhaite régler ma note" (I would like to settle my

bill). Most hotels have a check-out time, so ensure you're within this timeframe.

2. **Review the Bill**: The hotel staff will provide you with your final bill, which includes charges for your room and any additional expenses such as room service or minibar items. Take a moment to review the bill carefully, ensuring that all charges are accurate.

3. **Payment**: Pay the bill using your preferred method. You can settle it with cash or by credit card. If you're using a credit card, hand it over, and the staff will process the payment. Be sure to double-check the receipt for any added gratuity or service charges.

4. **Check-Out Time**: It's essential to adhere to the hotel's check-out time to avoid any additional charges. You can inquire about the check-out time by asking, "Quelle est l'heure de départ?" (What is the check-out time?). Plan your morning accordingly to ensure a stress-free departure.

5. **Return the Key**: Before leaving, return your room key to the front desk. Express your gratitude by saying, "Merci et au revoir" (Thank you and goodbye). This leaves a positive impression, and you may consider leaving a tip for the staff if you received exceptional service.

ASKING ABOUT PRICES AND AMENITIES

Inquiring About Room Prices: When you want to know the prices of the available rooms, you can politely ask, "Pouvez-vous me donner les tarifs des chambres, s'il vous plaît ?" (Can you please give me the room rates?). The hotel staff will provide you with a breakdown of the room types and their respective prices.

Asking About Included Amenities: To understand what amenities are included in your stay, you can inquire, "Quels sont les équipements inclus dans la chambre ?" (What amenities are included in the room?). This helps you know if services like breakfast, Wi-Fi, or access to the gym are part of the package.

Additional Amenities: If you're interested in specific amenities, such as a pool or spa, you can ask, "Avez-vous une piscine / un spa ?" (Do you have a pool / spa?). This helps you determine if the hotel offers the facilities you desire.

Parking Fees: If you have a vehicle and need parking, ask, "Y a-t-il des frais de stationnement ?" (Are there parking fees?). This ensures you're aware of any additional costs.

MAKING INFORMED CHOICES:

Comparing Room Types: When presented with various room options, take your time to compare. You can ask, "Pouvez-vous me décrire les différences entre les types de chambres ?" (Can you describe the differences between the room types?). This helps you make an informed decision based on your preferences and needs.

Considering Location: To make the best choice, consider the hotel's location in relation to your planned activities. You can say, "Pouvez-vous m'indiquer la proximité de l'hôtel aux attractions locales ?" (Can you tell me how close the hotel is to local attractions?). This helps ensure you stay in a convenient location.

Room Preferences: If you have specific preferences, such as a non-smoking room or a room with a view, communicate them by saying, "Je préférerais une chambre non-fumeur / avec vue." (I would prefer a non-smoking room / with a view). The hotel staff will do their best to accommodate your request.

Checking Reviews: In the age of online reviews, it's wise to research the hotel's reputation. You can mention, "J'ai lu de bonnes critiques en ligne sur votre hôtel" (I've read good reviews online about your hotel). This can be a conversation starter and may lead to additional insights from the staff.

Asking for Recommendations: If you're uncertain about your choice, don't hesitate to ask for recommendations. You can say, "Avez-vous des recommandations pour une expérience inoubliable ?" (Do you have any recommendations for an unforgettable experience?). Local knowledge can be invaluable.

MAKING A RESERVATION

Initiating the Reservation: When you're ready to make a reservation, it's polite to start with a greeting. You can say, "Bonjour, je voudrais faire une réservation, s'il vous plaît" (Hello, I would like to make a reservation, please).

Specify Dates and Duration: Clearly state your check-in and check-out dates along with the number of nights you plan to stay. For example, "Je voudrais réserver une chambre pour trois nuits, du [date d'arrivée] au [date de départ]" (I would like to book a room for three nights, from [arrival date] to [departure date]).

Number of Guests: Mention the number of guests who will be staying in the room. You can say, "Nous serons [number] personnes" (There will be [number] of us).

Room Preferences: If you have specific preferences, such as a double bed or a room with a view, kindly request them. You can say, "J'aimerais une chambre avec un lit double / vue sur [description]" (I would like a room with a double bed / a view of [description]).

Contact Information: Provide your contact information, including your name, phone number, and email address. Ensure the hotel can reach you if there are any questions or changes. You can say, "Voici mes coordonnées : [your contact information]" (Here are my contact details: [your contact information]).

Confirmation: Ask for confirmation of the reservation details. You can inquire, "Pouvez-vous confirmer ma réservation, s'il vous plaît ?" (Can you please confirm my reservation?).

SECURING YOUR STAY IN ADVANCE:

Deposit or Credit Card: To secure your reservation, the hotel may require a deposit or credit card information. They might say, "Nous aurons besoin d'une carte de crédit pour garantir la réservation" (We will need a credit card to guarantee the reservation).

Cancellation Policy: Inquire about the hotel's cancellation policy. You can ask, "Quelle est votre politique d'annulation ?" (What is your cancellation policy?). Understanding this helps you plan in case your travel plans change.

Confirmation Email: Request that the hotel sends you a confirmation email with all the reservation details. You can say, "Pourriez-vous m'envoyer un courrier électronique de confirmation, s'il vous plaît ?" (Could you please send me a confirmation email?).

Payment: Clarify whether you will be paying in advance or upon arrival. You can ask, "Dois-je payer à l'avance ou à l'arrivée ?" (Should I pay in advance or upon arrival?).

Check-In Procedures: It's a good idea to confirm the check-in time and any specific procedures, especially if you plan to arrive late. You can say, "Quelle est l'heure d'arrivée et les procédures de check-in ?" (What is the check-in time and check-in procedures?).

REPORTING A PROBLEM

Identifying the Issue: If you encounter a problem during your stay, it's crucial to identify the issue clearly. For instance, if there's a problem with the room's plumbing, say, "Il y a un problème avec la plomberie de la chambre" (There is an issue with the room's plumbing).

Contacting Reception: To report the problem, contact the hotel's reception or front desk immediately. You can do this by calling them or visiting in person. It's important to act promptly to resolve the issue.

Remaining Calm: When reporting the problem, remain calm and polite. This helps the hotel staff address the issue efficiently. You can say, "Excusez-moi, mais j'ai rencontré un problème dans ma chambre" (Excuse me, but I have encountered an issue in my room).

Providing Details: Offer specific details about the problem. Describe what you've observed or experienced, and if possible, show the staff the issue. This clarity will assist them in finding a solution.

Requesting Assistance: Politely request assistance or a resolution. You can say, "Pouvez-vous s'il vous plaît m'aider à résoudre ce problème ?" (Can you please help me resolve this issue?).

RESOLVING ISSUES WITH EASE:

Understanding the Hotel's Response: After reporting the problem, listen to the hotel staff's response. They may offer immediate assistance or provide a timeline for resolving the issue. It's important to understand their plan.

Alternative Accommodations: If the issue is severe and cannot be resolved quickly, inquire about the possibility of moving to another room or receiving alternative accommodations. You can ask, "Serait-il possible de changer de chambre ?" (Is it possible to change rooms?).

Maintaining Communication: Keep open communication with the hotel staff. If the problem persists or if you have concerns about the resolution, express them politely. Clear communication helps ensure your needs are met.

Documenting the Issue: If the issue significantly impacts your stay, consider documenting it with photographs or notes. This can be valuable if you need to escalate the matter or discuss it with management.

Seeking Compensation: In some cases, if the problem has caused significant inconvenience, you can politely discuss compensation with the hotel staff or management. This might include a discount or an offer for a future stay.

Feedback: After the issue is resolved, provide feedback to the hotel. Express gratitude for their assistance and share your thoughts on how the situation was handled. Constructive feedback can help improve the guest experience.

Remember, most hotels strive to provide excellent service, and issues can arise occasionally. Being polite, clear, and patient when reporting a problem will help you reach a satisfactory resolution with ease.

CHAPTER 4

FOOD AND DRINK

ORDERING FOOD AND DRINKS IN A RESTAURANT

1. **Greeting**: When you enter a restaurant, start with a polite greeting. You can say, "Bonjour" (Hello) or "Bonsoir" (Good evening) based on the time of day.
2. **Requesting a Table**: If you don't have a reservation, ask for a table by saying, "Pouvez-vous me donner une table pour [number] personnes, s'il vous plaît ?" (Can you give me a table for [number] people, please?).
3. **Menus**: When the waiter presents the menu, take your time to review it. If you need more time, you can say, "Je vais regarder le menu" (I will look at the menu).
4. **Asking Questions**: Don't hesitate to ask questions about the menu. If you're unsure about a dish, you can say, "Pouvez-vous m'expliquer ce que c'est ?" (Can you explain what this is?). This helps you make informed choices.
5. **Placing an Order**: When you're ready to order, say, "Je voudrais [dish or drink]" (I would like [dish or drink]). For example, "Je voudrais un verre de vin rouge" (I would like

a glass of red wine).

6. **Special Requests**: If you have dietary restrictions or specific preferences, communicate them clearly. For instance, "Je suis végétarien(ne), avez-vous des options végétariennes ?" (I am vegetarian, do you have vegetarian options?).

7. **Confirming**: After placing your order, the waiter may repeat it for confirmation. Listen carefully and confirm by saying, "Oui, c'est ça" (Yes, that's correct) or "Exactement" (Exactly).

8. **Drinks**: When ordering drinks, specify the type and size. For example, "Une grande bouteille d'eau gazeuse, s'il vous plaît" (A large bottle of sparkling water, please).

DINING WITH CONFIDENCE:

1. **Table Manners**: Familiarize yourself with basic table manners, such as using utensils appropriately and maintaining good posture while dining.

2. **Enjoying the Meal**: Savor your meal and the dining experience. Express appreciation by saying, "C'est délicieux, merci !" (It's delicious, thank you!).

3. **Dress Code**: Respect the restaurant's dress code, if applicable. Dressing appropriately contributes to a positive dining experience.

4. **Tipping**: In France, tipping is common but not mandatory. You can leave a tip by rounding up the bill or leaving a small amount for good service. Saying, "C'était excellent, gardez la monnaie" (It was excellent, keep the change) is a polite way to tip.

5. **Being Courteous**: Be courteous to the restaurant staff and

fellow diners. Avoid speaking too loudly and using your phone at the table.

6. **Understanding the Bill**: When you're ready to pay, request the bill by saying, "L'addition, s'il vous plaît" (The bill, please). Review the bill for accuracy before paying.

7. **Leaving**: After paying, you can thank the staff by saying, "Merci et au revoir" (Thank you and goodbye). Leave the restaurant with a courteous farewell.

READING A MENU

When dining in a French restaurant, one of the most enjoyable and rewarding experiences is exploring the culinary delights the menu has to offer. However, navigating a menu in a foreign language can sometimes be a challenge.

1. **Understanding Sections**: Menus are often divided into sections such as appetizers, mains, and desserts. Start by understanding the layout and sections of the menu.

2. **Dish Names**: Pay attention to the names of dishes. Some may be self-explanatory, while others may require further explanation.

3. **Ingredients and Descriptions**: Most menus provide descriptions of dishes, including key ingredients. Look for keywords like "poulet" (chicken), "poisson" (fish), "boeuf" (beef), and "légumes" (vegetables) to identify the primary components.

4. **Allergen Information**: Some menus may include allergen

information or symbols to indicate if a dish contains common allergens like nuts or gluten. Be sure to check for these if you have dietary restrictions.

5. **Price**: Pay attention to the prices listed next to each dish. This helps you make choices that align with your budget.

DECIPHERING CULINARY DELIGHTS:

Once you've mastered the basics of reading a menu, it's time to delve deeper into the world of culinary delights. From local specialties to unique ingredients and flavor combinations, French cuisine offers a treasure trove of tastes waiting to be explored

1. **Exploring Local Specialties**: If you're dining in a region known for specific dishes, consider trying local specialties. Ask the waiter for recommendations by saying, "Pouvez-vous me recommander un plat local ?" (Can you recommend a local dish?).

2. **Adventurous Tastes**: Dining can be an adventure, so don't hesitate to try something new. Look for unique ingredients or preparation methods, and be open to exploration.

3. **Asking Questions**: If you're unsure about a dish, don't hesitate to ask the waiter for more details. You can say, "Pouvez-vous me dire ce que contient ce plat ?" (Can you tell me what this dish contains?). This ensures you know exactly what you're ordering.

4. **Balancing Your Meal**: Consider balancing your meal by including a variety of flavors and ingredients. For example, if you choose a rich main course, opt for a lighter appetizer or dessert.

5. **Local Beverages**: Explore local beverages, such as wines, beers, or non-alcoholic options. Ask for recommendations to complement your meal.

6. **Sharing Dishes**: In some restaurants, sharing dishes is common. You can inquire, "Pouvons-nous partager ce plat ?" (Can we share this dish?). Sharing allows you to taste multiple items.

7. **Enjoying the Experience**: Dining is not just about the food; it's also about the experience. Take your time, savor each bite, and appreciate the ambiance of the restaurant.

8. **Feedback**: After your meal, consider providing feedback to the staff. If you enjoyed a particular dish, let them know. Constructive feedback helps improve the restaurant's offerings.

ASKING ABOUT DIETARY RESTRICTIONS

1. **Polite Inquiry**: When dining in a restaurant and you or your dining companion have dietary restrictions, it's essential to communicate them clearly and politely. You can begin by saying, "J'ai des restrictions alimentaires" (I have dietary restrictions).

2. **Specific Allergies**: If you or someone at your table has specific allergies, state them clearly. For instance, you can say, "Je suis allergique aux noix" (I am allergic to nuts).

3. **Vegetarian or Vegan Preferences**: If you're vegetarian or vegan, express your dietary preference by saying, "Je suis végétarien(ne)" (I am vegetarian) or "Je suis végétalien(ne)" (I am vegan).

46

4. **Gluten-Free**: For those who need gluten-free options, you can say, "J'ai besoin d'options sans gluten" (I need gluten-free options).

5. **Lactose Intolerance**: If you're lactose intolerant, communicate this by saying, "Je suis intolérant(e) au lactose" (I am lactose intolerant).

6. **Religious Restrictions**: Some dietary restrictions are based on religious beliefs. For example, you can mention, "Je suis juif(ve) et je ne mange pas de porc" (I am Jewish and do not eat pork).

7. **Preferred Alternatives**: It's helpful to mention any preferred alternatives you'd like. For instance, if you're vegetarian and would like a vegetable-based dish, you can say, "J'aimerais un plat à base de légumes" (I would like a vegetable-based dish).

8. **Inquiring About Options**: After stating your dietary restriction, it's a good idea to ask, "Avez-vous des options qui conviennent à mes restrictions alimentaires ?" (Do you have options that cater to my dietary restrictions?). This allows the waiter to provide suitable recommendations.

9. **Allergen Cross-Contamination**: If you have severe allergies, you can also ask about measures to prevent cross-contamination. For example, "Pouvez-vous garantir l'absence de contamination croisée avec [allergen] ?" (Can you guarantee no cross-contamination with [allergen]?).

10. **Expressing Appreciation**: Always express your gratitude for their understanding and assistance. Saying, "Je vous remercie de prendre en compte mes restrictions alimentaires" (Thank you for accommodating my dietary restrictions) is a polite way to show appreciation.

By clearly communicating your dietary restrictions and prefer-ences to the restaurant staff, you ensure a safe and enjoyable dining experience that aligns with your needs. French restau-rants are generally accommodating and will do their best to provide suitable options.

TIPPING

Tipping, known as "service" in French, is a customary practice in France. While it's not obligatory, it is appreciated for good service. Here are some important points to consider when it comes to tipping in France:

1. **Service Charge Included**: In many restaurants in France, a service charge is already included in the bill. This is often indicated as "Service compris" or "Service inclus" on the menu or bill. In such cases, an additional tip is not expected, although it's still common to round up the bill or leave small change as a gesture of appreciation.

2. **Rounding Up**: If the service charge is not included, it's common to round up the bill as a tip. For example, if your bill is €38, you can round it up to €40 or €42 as a tip. Leaving small change or rounding up is a polite way to show your appreciation for good service.

3. **Le pourboire**: In France, a tip is often referred to as "le pourboire." If you want to leave a specific amount as a tip, you can say, "Laissez le pourboire" (Leave the tip).

4. **Cash Tips**: While many restaurants accept credit cards, it's often more convenient to leave tips in cash. Waitstaff

generally appreciate receiving tips directly in cash.

5. **Cafés and Bars**: In cafés and bars, it's customary to leave small change or round up the bill for service. For example, if you order a coffee for €2.50, you might leave €3.

6. **Taxis**: It's customary to round up taxi fares to the nearest euro or add a small tip for taxi drivers.

7. **Hotel Staff**: In hotels, it's common to tip hotel staff such as bellhops, concierges, and housekeepers. A small tip of €1 to €2 for bellhops and €1 per day for housekeepers is appreciated.

8. **Tour Guides**: If you take guided tours, it's polite to tip the guide if you're satisfied with their service. A tip of €2 to €5 per person is typical.

9. **Exceptional Service**: If you receive exceptional service or dining experiences, you can tip more generously, but it's not expected.

Remember that tipping practices can vary from place to place, and it's important to use your discretion based on the level of service you receive. In France, tipping is a gesture of appreciation for good service rather than an obligation. It's always polite to say "Merci" (Thank you) when leaving a tip, and your appreciation will be warmly received.

CHAPTER 5

SHOPPING

ASKING FOR PRICES

When you embark on a shopping adventure in France, it's not just about finding that perfect item; it's also about understanding the prices and costs associated with your purchases.

Asking for Prices:

1. **Greeting and Approach**: Your shopping journey often begins with a greeting. As you enter a store or boutique, it's polite to start with a warm "Bonjour" (Hello) or "Bonsoir" (Good evening), depending on the time of day. This sets a positive tone for your interaction.

2. **Expressing Interest**: When you spot an item that catches your eye and you wish to know its price, the key phrase is "Combien ça coûte ?" (How much does this cost?). Pointing to the item while asking is a common gesture that communicates your interest clearly.

3. **Inquiring About Multiple Items**: In some cases, you might be considering several items. To inquire about the prices of all these items, you can politely request, "Pouvez-vous me donner les prix de ces articles ?" (Can you give me the prices of these items?). This allows you to make an informed decision based on your budget.

4. **Discounts and Sales**: Bargain hunters take note! If you want to find out if there are any discounts or ongoing sales, a useful phrase is "Y a-t-il des réductions ou des soldes en ce moment ?" (Are there any discounts or sales currently?). Knowing about discounts can help you make savvy purchasing decisions.

5. **Negotiation**: In certain markets or with particular vendors, haggling over the price is not just a possibility; it's an expected part of the shopping experience. You can initiate negotiation by politely asking, "Puis-je négocier le prix ?" (Can I negotiate the price?). Be prepared for a friendly back-and-forth to reach a mutually agreeable price.

INQUIRING ABOUT COSTS:

1. **Asking About Total Costs**: If you're considering multiple items and want to know the total cost of your potential purchases, you can inquire, "Quel serait le coût total ?" (What would be the total cost?). This is particularly helpful when planning your budget.

2. **Additional Costs**: It's essential to be aware of any additional costs that may be associated with your purchase. These could include taxes, shipping fees, or any other fees specific to the store or product. Politely ask, "Y a-t-il des coûts supplémentaires, comme des taxes ?" (Are there any

additional costs, like taxes?). This ensures that there are no surprises at the checkout.

3. **Payment Methods**: Knowing the accepted payment methods is crucial for a smooth transaction. To inquire about this, you can ask, "Quels sont les modes de paiement acceptés ?" (What are the accepted payment methods?). Whether it's cash, credit cards, or mobile payments, being prepared with the right payment method ensures a hassle-free shopping experience.

4. **Returns or Exchanges**: Understanding the store's policy regarding returns or exchanges is essential, especially if you have any concerns about the items you're purchasing. You can politely ask, "Quelle est votre politique de retour ou d'échange ?" (What is your return or exchange policy?). This information can be valuable in case you need to make changes to your purchases.

5. **Receipts**: Lastly, if you decide to make a purchase, requesting a receipt is a prudent practice. You can say, "Puis-je avoir un reçu, s'il vous plaît ?" (Can I have a receipt, please?). Receipts serve as proof of purchase and can be helpful for record-keeping, warranty claims, or potential returns.

6. **Haggling**: In specific markets or with certain vendors, haggling or negotiating the price is not only acceptable but also expected. To initiate negotiations, you can inquire, "Est-ce que le prix est négociable ?" (Is the price negotiable?). Be prepared for friendly back-and-forth interactions to reach a mutually satisfactory price.

By mastering the art of asking for prices and inquiring about costs while shopping in France, you'll be well-equipped to make informed decisions, stay within your budget, and enjoy a rewarding shopping experience.

TRYING ON CLOTHES

1. **Selecting Items to Try**: Begin by selecting the clothing items you'd like to try on. You can say, "Je voudrais essayer ces vêtements, s'il vous plaît" (I would like to try on these clothes, please). Hand the selected items to the store assistant if they are assisting you.

2. **Fitting Rooms**: Most stores have fitting rooms where you can try on clothes. You can ask, "Où sont les cabines d'essayage ?" (Where are the fitting rooms?). The store assistant will guide you to the fitting area.

3. **Limit on Items**: Some stores may have limits on the number of items you can take into the fitting room at once. It's a good idea to ask if there are any restrictions, like, "Combien d'articles puis-je emmener à la cabine d'essayage à la fois ?" (How many items can I take to the fitting room at once?).

4. **Trying on Comfortably**: Once inside the fitting room, take your time trying on each item. If you need different sizes, don't hesitate to ask the store assistant for assistance.

5. **Assistance**: If you need a different size, color, or style, you can politely request, "Pouvez-vous me trouver une taille/une couleur/un style différent(e) ?" (Can you find me a different size/color/style?).

6. **Evaluating the Fit**: While trying on clothes, assess how they fit. Pay attention to comfort, length, and overall appearance. Don't hesitate to step out of the fitting room

to use a mirror or ask for a second opinion.

Finding the Perfect Fit:

1. **Comfort**: The perfect fit starts with comfort. Make sure the clothing feels comfortable and allows you to move freely. If it's too tight or too loose, it may not be the right fit.
2. **Length and Proportions**: Pay attention to the length of pants, sleeves, and skirts. Ensure they are in proportion to your body. For example, pants should graze the top of your shoes.
3. **Shoulder Seams**: Check that shoulder seams sit at the edge of your shoulders. If they're too far in or too far out, the fit may not be right.
4. **Waist and Hips**: For bottoms like pants or skirts, ensure they fit comfortably around your waist and hips without gaping or feeling too tight.
5. **Tailoring**: Keep in mind that tailoring can be an option if you find a piece you love but it needs slight adjustments. Inquire about the possibility of alterations if needed.
6. **Walking and Movement**: Don't forget to walk, sit, and move while trying on clothes. Ensure that the fit allows for ease of movement without restrictions.
7. **Feedback**: If you're shopping with a friend or family member, ask for their feedback on how the clothes fit. A second opinion can be valuable.
8. **Ask for Assistance**: If you're unsure about the fit, don't hesitate to ask the store assistant for advice. They can provide insights and recommendations.

NEGOTIATING

When you step into a market or boutique in France, you have the opportunity to engage in one of the most intriguing aspects of shopping – negotiating and haggling for the best deal. While this practice might seem unfamiliar or even intimidating to some, it's an integral part of the shopping experience in many places in France.

Negotiating:

1. **Greeting and Establishing Rapport**: Begin your negotiation with a warm greeting and a friendly smile. Establishing a positive rapport with the seller can set the tone for a successful negotiation. You can start with a polite "Bonjour" (Hello) or "Bonsoir" (Good evening) depending on the time of day.

2. **Expressing Interest**: Express your genuine interest in the item you wish to purchase. You can say, "Cela m'intéresse beaucoup" (I'm very interested in this). This shows the seller that you are a serious buyer.

3. **Asking for the Initial Price**: Politely ask for the initial price by saying, "Combien coûte cet article ?" (How much does this item cost?). This allows you to gauge the starting point for negotiations.

4. **Listening Actively**: When the seller provides the initial price, listen carefully. Maintain eye contact and show that you are attentive to their response. This demonstrates respect for their perspective.

5. **Proposing Your Price**: Make a counteroffer by proposing a price that you believe is reasonable but lower than the

initial price. You can say, "Je vous propose [your price] euros" (I offer you [your price] euros). Be prepared for a back-and-forth negotiation.

6. **Justifying Your Offer**: Provide reasons for your offer, such as pointing out any minor flaws or defects in the item, mentioning similar prices you've seen elsewhere, or explaining your budget constraints.

7. **Remaining Patient and Polite**: Patience is key in negotiations. Remain polite and respectful throughout the process, even if the seller initially declines your offer. Negotiations in France are often a courteous exchange.

8. **Meeting in the Middle**: Be open to compromise. The seller may make a counteroffer, and you can work toward a price that both parties find acceptable.

HAGGLING FOR THE BEST DEAL:

1. **Knowing Your Limits**: Before entering negotiations, establish your upper limit or the maximum price you're willing to pay. This ensures that you don't overspend in the heat of the moment.

2. **Researching Prices**: Do some research beforehand to get a sense of the typical price range for the item you want to purchase. Knowledge of market prices can be a powerful negotiation tool.

3. **Inspecting the Item**: Thoroughly inspect the item you're interested in. Check for any defects or imperfections that you can use as negotiating points.

4. **Walking Away**: If negotiations reach a standstill and the seller is unwilling to meet your desired price, don't be afraid to walk away. In some cases, this can lead to the

seller reconsidering their offer.

5. **Returning**: If you do walk away and later decide to return to make the purchase, approach the seller with a reasonable offer based on your initial negotiations. This can often lead to a successful deal.

6. **Persistence with Politeness**: Persistence can pay off, but always maintain a polite and respectful demeanor. Building a positive relationship with the seller can lead to better deals in the future.

Negotiating and haggling for the best deal in France is a time-honored tradition, and it can be a rewarding and enjoyable part of your shopping experience.

PAYING FOR GOODS

After successful negotiations and finding the perfect items, the final steps of your shopping journey in France involve paying for your goods and settling your shopping bill.

Paying for Goods:

1. **Selecting Payment Method**: Start by selecting your pre-ferred payment method. In France, you can commonly use cash, credit cards, or mobile payment apps like Apple Pay or Google Pay.

2. **Payment Verification**: If you're using a credit card, the cashier will ask you to insert your card into the chip reader or swipe it if necessary. They may also ask for a PIN or a signature to verify the transaction.

3. **Currency**: When using cash, make sure you have the correct currency. In France, the Euro (€) is the official currency. Ensure that you have enough denominations to cover your bill.

4. **Digital Payments**: If you prefer mobile payment apps, ensure that your smartphone is ready, and your preferred payment method is set up. You may need to use a QR code or tap the device on a contactless payment terminal.

5. **Asking for a Receipt**: It's a good practice to ask for a receipt by saying, "Puis-je avoir un reçu, s'il vous plaît ?" (Can I have a receipt, please?). Receipts serve as proof of purchase and can be useful for record-keeping or potential returns.

SETTLING YOUR SHOPPING BILL:

1. **Reviewing the Bill**: Before making the payment, take a moment to review the bill. Ensure that all the items you intended to purchase are listed, and the prices are accurate.

2. **Verifying Additional Costs**: If there are any additional costs, such as taxes or service charges, make sure they are correctly calculated and included in the total.

3. **Payment Process**: Once you are satisfied with the bill, proceed with the payment method you've selected. Follow the instructions provided by the cashier or payment terminal.

4. **Receipt Confirmation**: After completing the payment, the cashier will provide you with a receipt. Verify that the receipt includes the date, store details, and the purchased items.

5. **Thanking and Departing**: Express your gratitude with a simple "Merci" (Thank you) to the cashier or store staff. You can also say, "Au revoir" (Goodbye) as you leave the

store.

6. **Checking Change**: If you paid with cash and received change, count it to ensure accuracy. Mistakes can happen, so it's always a good idea to double-check.

7. **Retaining the Receipt**: Keep the receipt in a safe place, especially if you plan to make returns or need to keep track of your expenses during your trip.

8. **Shopping Bags**: If you've made multiple purchases and need shopping bags, you can ask for them by saying, "Puis-je avoir des sacs, s'il vous plaît ?" (Can I have some bags, please?).

By following these steps and being attentive to the payment process, you can confidently settle your shopping bill and ensure that you have everything you need for a successful shopping experience.

CHAPTER 6

SIGHTSEEING

ASKING ABOUT ATTRACTIONS

Sightseeing in France is an enchanting journey filled with historic landmarks, cultural treasures, and breathtaking natural beauty. To make the most of your sightseeing adventures, it's essential to know how to ask about attractions and discover the points of interest that pique your curiosity.

Asking About Attractions:

1. **Greeting and Approach**: When inquiring about attractions, begin with a friendly greeting. You can say, "Bonjour" (Hello) or "Bonsoir" (Good evening) depending on the time of day.

2. **Expressing Interest**: Express your interest in exploring the local attractions by saying, "Je suis intéressé(e) à voir les attractions locales" (I am interested in seeing the local attractions).

3. **Asking for Recommendations**: You can ask for recommen-

dations by saying, "Pouvez-vous me recommander des attractions à visiter ici ?" (Can you recommend attractions to visit here?). Locals or tourist information centers are excellent sources for suggestions.

4. **Specific Inquiries**: If you have specific attractions in mind, you can ask directly, "Où puis-je trouver [attraction name] ?" (Where can I find [attraction name]?).

5. **Operating Hours**: Inquire about the operating hours of attractions by asking, "Quels sont les horaires d'ouverture de [attraction name] ?" (What are the opening hours of [attraction name]?).

DISCOVERING POINTS OF INTEREST:

1. **Research**: Before your trip, conduct research to identify the points of interest that align with your interests and preferences. Online travel guides, books, and apps can be valuable resources.

2. **Tourist Information Centers**: Visit local tourist information centers for brochures, maps, and up-to-date information about points of interest in the area.

3. **Asking Locals**: Engage with locals and seek their recommendations. They often have insights into hidden gems and lesser-known attractions.

4. **Guided Tours**: Consider joining guided tours or excursions to discover points of interest. Tour guides provide valuable insights and historical context.

5. **Online Resources**: Utilize online resources such as travel websites and forums where fellow travelers share their experiences and recommendations.

6. **Map Apps**: Use map apps like Google Maps to locate nearby

points of interest and get directions to them.

7. **Local Events**: Check if there are any local events, festivals, or exhibitions happening during your visit. These can provide unique opportunities for exploration.

8. **Cultural Centers**: Visit cultural centers, museums, and galleries to learn about the cultural heritage and artistic treasures of the region.

9. **Historical Sites**: Explore historical sites, including castles, cathedrals, and archaeological sites, to immerse yourself in the region's history.

10. **Natural Wonders**: Discover the natural beauty of the area by exploring parks, gardens, lakes, and scenic viewpoints.

BUYING TICKETS

1. **Selecting the Attraction**: Begin by choosing the cultural attraction or site you wish to visit. Once you've made your selection, it's time to purchase tickets.

2. **Ticket Counter**: Approach the ticket counter or entrance of the cultural site. If you're unsure where to buy tickets, you can politely ask, "Où puis-je acheter des billets ?" (Where can I buy tickets?).

3. **Ticket Types**: Inquire about the types of tickets available, including options for adults, children, students, and seniors. You can ask, "Quels sont les types de billets disponibles ?" (What types of tickets are available?).

4. **Pricing**: Ask about ticket prices by saying, "Combien coûtent les billets ?" (How much do the tickets cost?). Make sure to confirm the prices for your specific age group or

category.

5. **Discounts**: In some cases, there may be discounts for students, seniors, or large groups. Inquire about any available discounts by asking, "Y a-t-il des réductions disponibles ?" (Are there any discounts available?).

6. **Payment Methods**: Ask about the accepted payment methods at the ticket counter. Ensure that you have the appropriate form of payment, whether it's cash, credit card, or mobile payment.

7. **Receipt**: After purchasing tickets, request a receipt by saying, "Puis-je avoir un reçu, s'il vous plaît ?" (Can I have a receipt, please?). Receipts can be useful for record-keeping.

GAINING ACCESS TO CULTURAL TREASURES:

1. **Ticket Inspection**: After purchasing your tickets, be prepared for a ticket inspection at the entrance to the cultural site. Keep your tickets easily accessible.

2. **Security Check**: Some cultural sites may have security checks. Be prepared to go through metal detectors or have your bags inspected. Follow any security procedures in place.

3. **Timed Entry**: If the cultural site operates on timed entry or reservation systems, make sure to arrive at the specified time to gain access. Late arrivals may affect your entry.

4. **Guided Tours**: If guided tours are available, consider joining one to gain deeper insights into the cultural treasures. You can ask, "Y a-t-il des visites guidées disponibles ?" (Are guided tours available?).

5. **Visitor Information**: Check for visitor information or

information boards within the cultural site. These often provide historical context and details about the treasures you're about to explore.

6. **Respect Cultural Etiquette**: While enjoying cultural treasures, be respectful of any rules or guidelines in place. Some sites may have restrictions on photography or require quiet behavior.

7. **Audio Guides**: Some cultural sites offer audio guides in multiple languages. Inquire about the availability of audio guides if you prefer a self-guided tour.

8. **Exhibits and Displays**: Take your time to explore exhibits and displays. Read informational plaques and immerse yourself in the cultural significance of the treasures.

9. **Interaction**: In some interactive exhibits, you may be able to touch or engage with certain elements. Ensure that you follow any instructions provided by the site.

GETTING A TOUR GUIDE

When you're planning to explore cultural sites or historical landmarks in France, hiring a tour guide can greatly enhance your experience. Tour guides are knowledgeable experts who can provide valuable insights, historical context, and engaging stories related to the places you visit.

1. **Finding a Tour Guide**:

· **Official Tour Guides**: In many popular tourist destinations, you'll find official tour guides licensed by local authorities or tourism organizations. These guides are typically highly trained and knowledgeable about the specific region or site.

- **Private Tour Guides**: If you prefer a more personalized experience, you can hire a private tour guide. These guides can tailor the tour to your interests and schedule.
- **Tour Companies**: Many tour companies offer guided tours with experienced guides. Research and book tours in advance through reputable companies.

1. **Benefits of Having a Tour Guide**:

- **In-Depth Knowledge**: Tour guides provide detailed information about the history, architecture, and significance of the site you're visiting.
- **Engaging Narratives**: They can make the history come alive with engaging stories and anecdotes.
- **Efficient Navigation**: Guides can help you navigate through crowded sites efficiently, ensuring you don't miss key attractions.
- **Language Assistance**: If you're not fluent in French, a bilingual guide can bridge the language gap and enhance your understanding.

1. **Booking a Tour**:

- **Advance Booking**: It's advisable to book guided tours in advance, especially during peak tourist seasons when availability may be limited.
- **Group Tours**: Many sites offer group tours at scheduled times. You can join one of these tours by purchasing tickets at the site.

1. **Communication**:

- **Specify Your Interests**: When booking a tour, communicate your specific interests and preferences to the tour guide or company. This allows them to tailor the tour to your liking.
- **Ask Questions**: During the tour, don't hesitate to ask questions or request more information about aspects that intrigue you.

Enhancing Your Tour Experience:

1. **Active Participation**:

- **Engage with the Guide**: Interact with your tour guide by asking questions and sharing your thoughts. This fosters a dynamic learning experience.
- **Take Notes**: Consider bringing a notebook or using your smartphone to take notes about interesting facts or insights shared by the guide.

1. **Respectful Behavior**:

- **Follow Rules**: Respect any rules or guidelines set by the tour guide and the site you're visiting, such as rules regarding photography or noise levels.
- **Be Punctual**: Arrive on time for the tour to ensure that you don't miss any important information.

1. **Appreciation**:

- **Show Appreciation**: If you find the tour informative and enjoyable, it's customary to show appreciation to the tour guide. You can do this through a tip or a simple "Thank you" at the end of the tour.

1. **Exploration on Your Own**:

· **After the Tour**: Once the guided tour concludes, take the time to explore the site on your own if it allows. This allows you to revisit specific areas of interest or take photographs at your own pace.

1. **Further Learning**:

· **Reading and Research**: If a particular historical site or topic piques your interest, consider reading books or conducting online research to deepen your understanding.

1. **Group Interaction**:

· **Interact with Fellow Tourists**: Don't hesitate to strike up conversations with fellow tourists during group tours. You may exchange travel tips and experiences.

1. **Feedback**: Provide constructive feedback to the tour guide or tour company after the tour. This can help them improve their services and tailor future tours to the interests of visitors.

By considering these tips, you can make the most of your guided tour experiences in France. Whether you're exploring iconic landmarks, museums, or hidden gems, a knowledgeable tour guide can transform your visit into an educational and memorable adventure.

ASKING FOR INFORMATION

While exploring a new place in France, seeking information is essential to enhance your understanding of the culture, history, and attractions. Whether you're in a museum, historic site, or simply wandering through a neighborhood, knowing how to ask for information is valuable.

1. **Polite Inquiry**: When you approach someone for information, begin with a polite greeting such as "Bonjour" (Hello) or "Excusez-moi" (Excuse me). This sets a courteous tone for your interaction.
2. **Specific Questions**:

- **Location**: If you need directions or want to know where a particular place is, you can ask, "Où est [place name] ?" (Where is [place name]?).
- **Operating Hours**: For information about the opening and closing hours of a museum, restaurant, or store, inquire with "Quels sont les horaires d'ouverture ?" (What are the opening hours?).
- **Recommendations**: When seeking recommendations, you can ask, "Pouvez-vous me recommander un bon restaurant près d'ici ?" (Can you recommend a good restaurant nearby?).
- **Historical Information**: If you're at a historic site, inquire about its history by saying, "Pouvez-vous me raconter

l'histoire de cet endroit ?" (Can you tell me the history of this place?).

1. **Language Barrier**: If you're not fluent in French, it's helpful to have a few key phrases and questions written down or saved on your phone. Many locals appreciate your effort to communicate in their language.
2. **Listening Actively**: When someone provides information, actively listen and show appreciation with nods or expressions of understanding. This encourages open and informative conversations.

GATHERING INSIGHTS FROM LOCALS:

One of the most enriching aspects of traveling in France is interacting with locals. Their insights, recommendations, and stories can provide you with a deeper understanding of the culture and the best experiences the region has to offer.

1. **Openness and Respect**: Approach interactions with locals with an open mind and respectful demeanor. Show genuine interest in their culture and perspectives.
2. **Local Gathering Spots**: Visit local gathering spots such as cafes, markets, and community events. These places are excellent for striking up conversations with residents.
3. **Language**: While many French people speak English, especially in tourist areas, learning a few basic French phrases can go a long way in fostering positive interactions. Locals often appreciate the effort to speak their language.
4. **Initiating Conversations**:

- **Compliments**: Start conversations with compliments about the local area or their culture. For example, you can say, "J'adore votre belle ville" (I love your beautiful city).
- **Questions**: Ask open-ended questions about their experiences and recommendations. For instance, "Quels sont les endroits que vous aimez visiter ici ?" (What are the places you like to visit here?).

1. **Local Cuisine**: Food is a fantastic conversation starter. Ask locals about their favorite local dishes and where to find the best ones.
2. **Participate in Local Activities**: Engage in local activities, workshops, or festivals. These experiences often lead to interactions with enthusiastic residents who are eager to share their traditions.
3. **Local Guides**: Consider hiring local guides or joining guided tours led by residents. They can provide insider insights and stories that you might not find in guidebooks.
4. **Social Media and Online Communities**: Join social media groups or online travel forums related to France. These platforms are excellent for connecting with locals and seeking recommendations.
5. **Express Gratitude**: After engaging with locals and receiving insights or assistance, express your gratitude with a sincere "Merci" (Thank you).

CHAPTER 7

EMERGENCY PHRASES

CALLING FOR HELP

I n any travel situation, it's crucial to know how to call for help in case of emergencies. In France, as in many countries, the emergency number is 112. This number can be dialed for police, medical, or fire emergencies.

1. **Dialing 112**: To make an emergency call, simply dial 112 from your phone. It works on all phones, even if you don't have a local SIM card.
2. **Language**: While operators may speak English, it's a good idea to know some essential phrases in French to communicate your emergency effectively.
3. **Stay Calm and Clear**: When making an emergency call, it's essential to stay calm and speak clearly. State the type of emergency and your location as accurately as possible.
4. **Phrase for Calling for Help**: To call for help, say, "À l'aide !" (Help!) or "C'est une urgence !" (It's an emergency!). This can quickly alert people nearby that

you need assistance.

5. **Providing Information**: After calling for help, provide the operator with the following information:

- Your name.
- Your location (address or landmark).
- The nature of the emergency (police, medical, or fire).
- Any additional details, such as the number of people involved or the severity of injuries.

RESPONDING TO URGENT SITUATIONS:

In urgent situations, your quick and appropriate response can make a significant difference.

1. **Stay Calm**: The first rule in responding to any emergency is to remain as calm as possible. Panic can hinder your ability to think clearly and take effective action.
2. **Assess the Situation**: Take a moment to assess the situation. Determine the nature and severity of the emergency.
3. **Ensure Safety**: Prioritize your safety and the safety of others. If the situation poses a risk to your well-being, move to a safe location if possible.
4. **Call for Help**: If the situation requires immediate assistance, dial 112 or the local emergency number. Provide accurate and detailed information to the operator.
5. **Administer First Aid**: If you have basic first-aid knowledge and it's safe to do so, provide first aid to any injured individuals while waiting for professional help to arrive.
6. **Alert Others**: If there are people nearby, alert them to the emergency and request assistance. In public places, you

can shout, "À l'aide !" (Help!).

7. **Follow Instructions**: If you're communicating with emergency responders or medical professionals, follow their instructions carefully. They are trained to provide guidance in critical situations.

8. **Document Details**: If possible, document the details of the emergency, such as the time it occurred, any injuries, and any actions taken. This information can be useful later for reporting or insurance purposes.

9. **Offer Comfort**: In situations involving others, offering comfort and reassurance can be valuable. Stay with individuals who need assistance and provide emotional support.

Remember that in emergencies, every second counts. Being prepared with the knowledge of how to call for help and respond appropriately can potentially save lives. It's also a good idea to familiarize yourself with local emergency services and resources in the area you're visiting to ensure a swift and effective response in urgent situations.

ASKING FOR MEDICAL ASSISTANCE

In case of a medical emergency or when you or someone you're with requires medical assistance in France, knowing how to ask for help is essential.

1. **Dialing Emergency Services**: For medical emergencies in France, dial the emergency number 112 or 15. These numbers connect you to medical services, including ambulance dispatch.

2. **Stay Calm**: Maintain a calm demeanor when making an emergency call. Clearly communicate the urgency of the situation and provide essential information.

3. **Essential Information**: When requesting medical assistance, provide the following information to the operator:

- Your name.
- The nature of the medical emergency (e.g., injury, illness, or specific symptoms).
- The location of the incident (address or landmark).
- The number of people involved.
- Any additional details that can help responders, such as allergies or chronic medical conditions.

1. **Phrase for Asking for Medical Help**: To request medical assistance, you can say, "J'ai besoin d'une ambulance, s'il vous plaît" (I need an ambulance, please) or simply "Au secours !" (Help!).

SEEKING HEALTHCARE SUPPORT:

In non-emergency situations, when you require medical care or advice in France, understanding how to seek healthcare support is important.

1. **Medical Facilities**: France has a well-developed healthcare system with hospitals, clinics, and pharmacies widely available. You can seek healthcare support at the following places:

- **Pharmacies**: For minor ailments and over-the-counter

medications, pharmacies are a convenient option. Look for the green cross sign.

· **Clinics**: Local clinics or "cabinets médicaux" provide general medical care for non-emergencies.
· **Hospitals**: For serious medical conditions or emergencies, hospitals offer comprehensive healthcare services.

1. **Health Insurance**: Ensure that you have valid health insurance coverage during your stay in France. European Health Insurance Cards (EHIC) or private travel insurance can provide financial support for medical expenses.
2. **Making Appointments**: To see a doctor or specialist, it's generally advisable to make an appointment in advance, although some clinics also accept walk-ins.
3. **Language**: While many medical professionals in France speak English, having basic medical phrases in French can be helpful. You can say:

· "J'ai besoin de voir un médecin" (I need to see a doctor).
· "Je ne me sens pas bien" (I don't feel well).
· "J'ai des douleurs ici" (I have pain here), indicating the affected area.

1. **Pharmacy Visits**:

· When visiting a pharmacy for non-prescription medications, describe your symptoms to the pharmacist, who can recommend appropriate products.
· Always bring a list of any medications you are currently taking, including their names and dosages.

1. **Clinic and Hospital Visits**:

- Provide details about your condition to the healthcare provider.
- Bring any relevant medical records or documents, such as prescriptions or previous medical history.

1. **Healthcare Costs**: Be prepared to pay for healthcare services or medications upfront, and then you can claim reimbursement from your insurance provider later.
2. **Emergency Care**: In case of a severe medical emergency, go directly to the nearest hospital or call emergency services (112 or 15). Emergency care is provided without regard to insurance coverage.
3. **Pharmacy Hours**: Be aware of pharmacy hours, as they may vary. Some pharmacies operate 24/7 on a rotating schedule to provide essential services during off-hours.

Familiarizing yourself with these guidelineswill help you confidently seek medical assistance and healthcare support when needed during your stay . Having a basic understanding of the healthcare system and local practices can help ensure a smoother experience in managing your health while abroad.

REPORTING A CRIME

In unfortunate situations where you witness or are a victim of a crime in France, knowing how to report it is essential for your safety and the safety of others.

1. **Emergency Services**: If you witness or are involved in a crime in progress or in a situation requiring immediate police assistance, dial the emergency number 112 or 17. These numbers connect you to the police.
2. **Stay Safe**: Ensure your safety and the safety of others before taking any action. If you can do so without risking harm, provide assistance to victims or witnesses.
3. **Stay Calm**: When reporting a crime, stay as calm as possible. Clearly and accurately describe the situation to the operator. Provide the following information:

- Your name.
- The nature of the crime (e.g., theft, assault, or vandalism).
- The location of the incident (address or landmark).
- A description of the suspect(s), if applicable.
- Any additional details that can help authorities respond effectively.

1. **Cooperate with Dispatch**: Follow the instructions provided by the emergency operator. They may ask you questions to gather more information or provide guidance on how to stay safe.
2. **Phrases for Reporting a Crime**: To report a crime, you can say, "Je veux signaler un crime" (I want to report a crime) or "Il y a eu un vol ici" (There has been a theft here).

COOPERATING WITH AUTHORITIES:

When law enforcement arrives to investigate a crime, cooperating with authorities is vital for their efforts to maintain safety and resolve the situation.

1. **Stay Calm and Compliant**: If law enforcement approaches you or asks for your cooperation, stay calm and comply with their requests. Follow their instructions promptly and respectfully.

2. **Identification**: Be prepared to provide identification, such as your passport or ID, if requested by law enforcement. It's important to carry your identification with you when traveling.

3. **Provide Information**: If you witnessed the crime or have information related to it, provide your statement to the police. Be truthful and as detailed as possible while recounting the events.

4. **Witness Testimony**: If you're asked to be a witness, cooperate fully. Your testimony may be crucial in helping authorities understand the circumstances of the crime.

5. **Legal Rights**: Familiarize yourself with your legal rights in France. You have the right to remain silent, and you can request legal representation if you are involved in a legal matter.

6. **Language Assistance**: If you're not fluent in French and need language assistance, you can request an interpreter or use a translation app to ensure clear communication.

7. **Documentation**: If you are asked to provide any documents, such as identification or witness statements, keep copies for your records.

8. **Legal Support**: If you believe you may require legal assistance, consider consulting with a lawyer. They can provide guidance on your rights and responsibilities.

9. **Report as Needed**: Continue to cooperate with authorities throughout the investigative process. If you have additional information or need to follow up, do so promptly.

GETTING TO THE POLICE STATION

If you need to visit a police station in France, it's essential to know how to get there safely and efficiently.

1. **Location**: Locate the nearest police station to your current location. You can ask locals for directions or use a map app on your phone to find the station's address.
2. **Transportation Options**: Depending on your location and the distance to the police station, you can choose from various transportation options:

- **Walking**: If the police station is nearby, consider walking if it's safe to do so.
- **Public Transport**: Use public transportation, such as buses or trams, to reach the station. Be sure to check schedules and routes in advance.
- **Taxi or Ride-Share**: If you prefer a convenient and direct option, you can hail a taxi or use a ride-sharing app like Uber.

1. **Ask for Directions**: Don't hesitate to ask locals or passersby for directions to the police station. Politeness goes a long way, so use phrases like "Excusez-moi, où est le commissariat de police le plus proche ?" (Excuse me, where is the nearest police station?).
2. **Safety**: Ensure your personal safety while traveling to the police station, especially if you're visiting due to a specific incident. If you feel uncomfortable or unsafe, consider requesting a police escort.

NAVIGATING LEGAL MATTERS:

Legal matters in a foreign country can be complex, and it's crucial to approach them with caution and understanding.

1. **Legal Assistance**: If you find yourself facing legal issues in France, it's advisable to consult with a lawyer who specializes in the relevant area of law. They can provide guidance on your rights and legal options.

2. **Language Barrier**: If you are not fluent in French, hiring a bilingual lawyer or an interpreter can facilitate effective communication with legal authorities.

3. **Documentation**: Keep all relevant documents and records related to your legal matter organized and accessible. This may include contracts, correspondence, or any evidence pertaining to your case.

4. **Police Reports**: If you've been involved in an incident requiring police intervention, request a copy of the police report for your records. It may be useful for legal proceedings.

5. **Consular Assistance**: If you are a foreign national facing legal issues in France, consider contacting your embassy or consulate for guidance and support. They can provide information on consular services available to you.

6. **Legal Processes**: Familiarize yourself with the legal processes specific to your situation. This may include understanding the steps involved in filing a complaint, pursuing a legal case, or resolving disputes.

7. **Representation**: If your legal matter requires court proceedings, you have the right to legal representation. Engage a lawyer to represent your interests and guide you

through the process.

8. **Mediation**: In some cases, mediation or alternative dispute resolution methods may be available to resolve legal disputes without going to court. Discuss these options with your lawyer if applicable.

9. **Adherence to Local Laws**: Ensure that you adhere to local laws and regulations during your stay in France. Ignorance of the law is not typically considered a valid defense.

Navigating legal matters can be complex, and it's essential to seek professional guidance and support when necessary.

APPENDIX

50 COMMONLY USEFUL PHRASES FOR TRAVELERS:

1. Bonjour – Hello
2. Bonsoir – Good evening
3. Bonne nuit – Good night
4. Salut – Hi / Bye (Informal)
5. Comment ça va ? – How are you?
6. Je m'appelle [Your Name] – My name is [Your Name]
7. Parlez-vous anglais ? – Do you speak English?
8. Oui – Yes
9. Non – No
10. S'il vous plaît – Please
11. Merci – Thank you
12. De rien – You're welcome
13. Excusez-moi – Excuse me
14. Où est... ? – Where is...?
15. Combien ça coûte ? – How much does it cost?
16. Pouvez-vous m'aider ? – Can you help me?
17. L'addition, s'il vous plaît – The check, please
18. Je ne comprends pas – I don't understand
19. Parlez plus lentement, s'il vous plaît – Speak more slowly,

please

20. Pouvez-vous répéter ? - Can you repeat that?
21. Oui, bien sûr - Yes, of course
22. Non, merci - No, thank you
23. Je voudrais... - I would like...
24. L'eau - Water
25. La nourriture - Food
26. La carte - Menu
27. Café - Coffee
28. Thé - Tea
29. Vin - Wine
30. Bière - Beer
31. Pain - Bread
32. Sel - Salt
33. Poivre - Pepper
34. Sucre - Sugar
35. Toilettes - Restrooms
36. Hôtel - Hotel
37. Chambre - Room
38. Clé - Key
39. Ouvert - Open
40. Fermé - Closed
41. Entrée - Entrance
42. Sortie - Exit
43. Urgence - Emergency
44. Médecin - Doctor
45. Pharmacie - Pharmacy
46. Police - Police
47. Aidez-moi - Help me
48. J'ai besoin d'aide - I need help
49. Où est la gare ? - Where is the train station?

50. Je suis perdu - I am lost

These phrases should prove very helpful during your travels in French-speaking regions.

Conclusion

As we bring this simple and easy guide on conversational French for travelers to a close, we want to express our heartfelt wishes for your upcoming journey. Traveling to a foreign land, especially one where the language may be unfamiliar, can be a thrilling and enriching experience. Armed with the knowledge and skills you've gained from this guide, you're well-prepared to embark on an unforgettable adventure in France and beyond.

Throughout this guide, we've explored the intricacies of the French language, from essential greetings and introductions to navigating daily situations such as dining, shopping, and exploring the beautiful sights. We've also delved into the crucial aspects of accommodation, ensuring that your stays in hotels or other lodgings are seamless and enjoyable.

As you prepare to explore the charming streets of Paris, the picturesque vineyards of Bordeaux, or the stunning landscapes of Provence, remember that language is not just a means of communication but a bridge to connect with the culture and people of your destination. Your willingness to embrace the French language, even in its simplest form, will open doors to enriching experiences and heartfelt connections with locals.

But beyond the language, traveling is an opportunity for personal growth and cultural enrichment. It's a chance to savor delectable cuisine, immerse yourself in art and history, and savor the beauty of diverse landscapes. It's a time to discover the unexpected, whether it's stumbling upon a quaint café in a hidden alley or striking up a conversation with a fellow traveler.

So, as you step into the unknown with your phrasebook in hand and a heart full of curiosity, remember that every encounter, every mispronounced word, and every small victory in understanding and being understood is a part of the incredible tapestry of travel. Cherish the moments, learn from them, and relish the unique stories you'll collect along the way.

Whether you're exploring the bustling markets of Marseille, gazing at the grandeur of the Palace of Versailles, or simply sipping a café au lait at a sidewalk café in Montmartre, may your journey be filled with wonder, joy, and the kind of memories that linger long after you've returned home.

Bon voyage, dear traveler! May your adventures be boundless, and may the world welcome you with open arms.

BON VOYAGE !!!!